The SPEAK ENGLISH, READ ENGLISH, WRITE ENGLISH ACTIVITY BOOK

for children and adults, A1 to A2

Copyright © 2024 Zigzag English / Lydia Winter

All rights reserved. No part of this publication may be reproduced or transmitted in any form without the written permission of the author.

ISBN: 978-1-914911-83-5

www.zigzagenglish.co.uk

OUR BOOKS FOR LEARNING ENGLISH

OUR DIALOGUE BOOKS FOR ADULTS:
50 Easy Everyday English Dialogues - A2-B1
50 Intermediate Everyday English Dialogues - B1-B2
50 more Intermediate Everyday English Dialogues - B1-B2
40 Advanced Everyday English Dialogues - B2-C1
40 Intermediate Business English Dialogues - B1-B2
40 Advanced Business English Dialogues - B2-C1

OUR ACTIVITY BOOKS FOR ADULTS AND CHILDREN:
The Speak English, Read English, Write English Activity Book - A1-A2 (easy)
The Speak English, Read English, Write English Activity Book - A2-B1 (lower intermediate)

OUR BILINGUAL BOOKS FOR CHILDREN (age 4-7) *with French, German, Spanish and Italian. Also available in English only (as Tony the Dog):*
English with Tony -1- Tony moves house
English with Tony -2- Tony is happy
English with Tony -3- Tony's Christmas
English with Tony -4- Tony's holiday
My Best Friend

OUR DIALOGUE BOOKS FOR CHILDREN (from beginner level):
I Speak English Too! - 1
I Speak English Too! – 2

OUR READING AND COMPREHENSION BOOKS FOR CHILDREN (from beginner level):
Read English with Zigzag - 1
Read English with Zigzag - 2
Read English with Zigzag - 3
Audiobook - Books 1 and 2

OUR READING, COMPREHENSION AND ACTIVITY BOOKS FOR CHILDREN
(from elementary level):
Read English with Ben - 1
Read English with Ben - 2
Read English with Ben - 3

OUR ACTIVITY BOOK FOR CHILDREN:
The Learn English Activity Book for Children – A1-A2

Dear Reader,

I hope you enjoy this activity book. Its aim is to help you consolidate your level of English while having fun.

You will need to look up some words in the dictionary - a vital skill for language learners.

Where a page has an asterisk *, you can check the solutions at the back of the book.

If you have any questions, or suggestions for improving the book, please email me at:
lydiawinter.zigzagenglish@gmail.com.
Suggestions for new books are always welcome.

The Zigzag English website is here:
www.zigzagenglish.co.uk
You can find out about our other books for adults and children, do some more English language activities and read the blog.

Please leave a review for this book. Thank you!

FIND THE RIGHT WORDS

Hi
I'm fine
How are you?
Bye
Good morning
What's up?
I'm okay
See you later
How've you been?
Not too bad
Catch you later
Take care
It's nice to meet you
Hey
How's it going?
Good to see you
It was nice to meet you
Very well thanks
So so

COMPLETE THE DIALOGUE

A: Hello.

You:

A: My name's Anna.

You:

A: It's nice to meet you.

You:

A: Where are you from?

You:

A: You speak good English!

You:

A: Are you busy? Do you have time for a coffee?

You:

A: Great. I'm hungry. Let's have something to eat too. What do you want to eat?

You:

A: That sounds good. Are there any good cafés or restaurants in this town?

You:

A: Oh no! It's half past one. My train's at two o'clock. I don't have time for lunch.

You:

A: Can we meet up another time? When are you free?

You:

A: Okay, great. Here's my phone number. Call me!

CONTINENTS *

1. Can you name all these continents?
2. How many start with the letter A?
3. Which is the largest and which is the second-largest?
4. Where can you find the most people?
5. Which is the flattest?
6. Are there more countries in Africa, Europe or Asia?
7. Which continent is the smallest country in the world in?
8. What do you call someone who's from Europe?
9. What's the best continent for speaking English?
10. Where do you live?

CHOOSE A WILD ANIMAL FOR EACH CONTINENT

sloth, deer, grizzly bear, kangaroo, panda, giraffe

Now choose one or two adjectives for each animal:

tall, fast, aggressive, fat, slow, rare, dangerous, cute, colourful, lazy, delicious, common, heavy, beautiful

Can you find any opposite adjectives?

How many of these animals have you seen? Were they in the wild or in a zoo?

ODD ONE OUT *

Which word is the odd one out?

1. lamb   goat   kitten   chick
2. fantastic   cute   boring   delicious
3. Japan   India   Egypt   South Korea
4. story   picture   photo   painting
5. climb   swim   jump   run
6. Brazil   New Zealand   Ireland   Canada
7. chicken   broccoli   pork   beef
8. kind   pretty   nice   friendly
9. bee   spider   wasp   butterfly
10. apple juice   wine   beer   lemonade
11. bike   bus   taxi   train
12. hit   kick   head   shoot
13. water   milk   whisky   custard
14. cow   fox   dog   pig
15. massive   large   enormous   gigantic
16. talk   speak   shout   say
17. shark   dolphin   whale   polar bear
18. t-shirt   trousers   jacket   jumper

ANDREW'S FAMILY - TRUE OR FALSE? *

I have a big family. I have three grandparents - one grandfather and two grandmothers. My dad's mother is ninety-eight now and her husband died fifteen years ago. They had six children, and my mum has an older sister and two younger brothers, so I have lots of aunts and uncles, and about twenty-five cousins.

My mum is in her late sixties and my dad is in his early seventies. My mum had me when she was thirty-five - I was her last child.

My older brother got married very young, but the marriage didn't last. He got divorced when he was only twenty-three and married again five years later. He has a son with his first wife and two daughters with his second wife (they're still together). His daughters get on very well with their half-brother. I learned from my brother's mistake and didn't get married until I was older.

My sister isn't married. She has an important job and travels all over the world for the company she works for. She says she never wanted children, but she's a very good aunt to my two boys. That's important to me because I lost my wife a few years ago, when my sons were teenagers. It was a very difficult time for all of us, but our family did everything they could to help.

My sons are both at university now. They come home every holiday. One of them has a lovely girlfriend and is already talking about getting married. I think he's much too young for that. I'd love to have grandchildren, but I can wait a few years.

1. Andrew is in his thirties.   T / F
2. He's married.   T / F
3. His father is older than his mother.   T / F
4. Andrew is a widower.   T / F
5. His sons are probably in their late twenties.   T / F
6. Andrew learned from his brother that getting married early is a good idea.   T / F
7. He has ten uncles and aunts and around twenty-five cousins.   T / F

YOUR FAMILY

Answer the questions:

1. How big is your family?
2. Are your grandparents still alive? How old are they?
3. How many cousins have you got? How often do you see them?
4. Do you have any brothers or sisters? Are they older or younger than you? Or are you an only child?
5. Do you still live with your parents?
6. Or do you live by yourself or with someone else?
7. Are you married? If you have any brothers or sisters, are they married?
8. Is anyone in your family divorced or widowed? (widowed = your husband or wife has died)
9. Do you have any children?
10. When do you think is the best age to get married?

HANDS

Find the right words:

bad
love
go
pray
you
hope
well done
agree
wish
friendship
come
goodbye

KIM'S GAME – REMEMBER THE VERBS

YOU HAVE 1 MINUTE TO LOOK AT THESE WORDS. THEN SHUT THE BOOK AND WRITE DOWN AS MANY OF THEM AS YOU CAN REMEMBER.

VERBS - ANSWER THE QUESTIONS

Use your imagination to answer these questions:

1) Why are the men fighting?
2) What are the two friends watching on television?
3) Why does Paul's grandfather need him to help him?
4) What are the teenage girls arguing about?
5) What has John forgotten? What is he trying to remember?
6) How far is Mary cycling today?
7) Which grandchild is Ian looking after this morning?
8) What is Anna's boss explaining to her?
9) What are you looking for?
10) Is there anything you need to ask me?

HOW OFTEN? - ADVERBS OF FREQUENCY

Choose the words you need to answer these questions:

1. How often do you eat out?
2. How often is someone rude to you?
3. How often do you have tea or coffee with a friend?
4. How often do you go away on holiday?
5. How often do you visit a castle?
6. How often do you have a bath or shower?
7. How often do you spend the night at a friend's house?
8. How often do you ride a bike?
9. How often do you have breakfast in your pyjamas?
10. How often do you work after 8 o'clock in the evening?
11. How often does someone give you a present?
12. How often do you feel tired at 11 o'clock in the morning?

not very often
normally
every day
three times a year
all the time
never
once a month
usually
most days
occasionally
always
quite often
twice a day
sometimes
hardly ever

HOW OFTEN? - 2

Life is busy and expensive. There's never enough time and money to do everything we want to do. For example, I love eating out, but my friends and family don't have time to go to a restaurant with me very often, so I only eat out about once a month, usually on a Saturday. I hardly ever go to a really good restaurant, because no-one I know likes spending lots of money on food.

Because I like food so much, I try to go the gym every day, after work. But to be honest I normally only go about three times a week. I always go swimming at the weekend, though. The company I work for has a badminton club, so I occasionally play badminton with a colleague at lunchtime.

I should probably eat and drink less and take more exercise. My parents tell me that all the time.

Now talk or write about how you spend your time. Try to use lots of adverbs of frequency.

WHAT TIME IS IT? *

In the UK and the United States people usually use the 12 hour clock.

MATCH THE TIMES:

It's a quarter past one   It's 9:10 - nine ten
It's ten to nine   It's 5:54 - five fifty-four
It's twenty-five past seven   It's 3:03 - three oh three
It's twenty to four   It's 7:25 - seven twenty-five
It's five past two   It's 1:15 - one fifteen
It's six minutes to six   It's 7 p.m. - seven p.m.
It's a quarter to eight   It's 8:50 - eight fifty
It's ten past nine   It's 7:45 - seven forty-five
It's half past five in the morning   It's 5:30 a.m. - five thirty a.m.
It's twelve o'clock / midnight   It's 2:05 - two oh five
It's three minutes past three   It's 3:40 - three forty
It's seven o'clock in the evening   It's 12 - twelve / midnight

- *What time is it?*
- *What time will it be in one hour and two minutes?*
- *What time was it half an hour ago?*
- *What time is it in London?*
- *What time is it in Sydney?*

WHAT TIME? *

Tom does the same things, at the same time, every Friday.
Use the present simple to say what time he does everything:

- He gets up at a quarter past seven. (or at seven fifteen.)
- He has a shower...

FLATSHARE

Young people often have to share a house or flat with people they don't know.

You have to live with one of:

- Someone who smokes
- Someone who plays the violin very badly for hours every day.
- Someone who uses the bathroom between 7 o'clock and 8 o'clock every morning.
- Someone who doesn't speak a word of your language or of English.
- Someone who comes home at midnight every night and then makes dinner and has a bath.
- Someone who never does any cleaning.
- Someone who wants to keep the heating on all night.
- Someone who often steals your food from the fridge.
- Someone who invites their four noisy friends round every evening.
- Someone with a large dog.

Which flatmate do you choose?

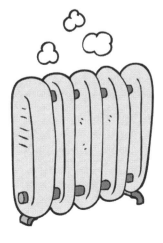

WHAT ARE THEY SAYING?

How are they feeling?
What are they saying or thinking?

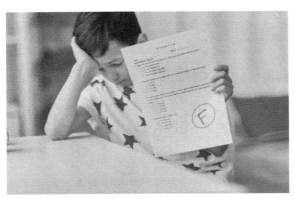

CHRISTMAS PRESENTS

It's almost Christmas. Choose presents for your friends and family.

Your brother (15):
Your sister (7):
Your mother (40):
Your father (44):
Your grandmother (73):
Your grandfather (71):
Your best friend Tom (12):
Your favourite teacher:
Your dog:

Choose from:
A big box of chocolates, a bottle of red wine, a plastic ball, a good book, a beautiful necklace, a family photo, a packet of sweets, a popular board game, a leather jacket.

CHOOSE!

You can have something, but you can't have everything.
So what do you choose?

- Cheese OR chocolate?
- Only white clothes OR only red clothes?
- A lovely big house with a swimming pool and no holidays OR 3 holidays a year and a tiny flat?
- You're always tired OR you're always angry?
- A pet snake OR a pet rat?
- You're good at everything and no-one likes you OR you're bad at everything and you have lots of friends?
- Flowers every day OR wine every day?
- A fun job with very little money OR a horrible job with lots of money?

Can you write 3 more?

-

-

-

THE COUNTRYSIDE – BIG OR SMALL?

BIG: **SMALL:**

mountain   hill

lake   pond

forest   wood

ocean   sea

NOT ENOUGH TIME

Amy doesn't like being a grown-up.

She's twenty-one. A few months ago she was a student. She got up at ten or eleven o'clock every day. She had breakfast in her pyjamas, watching funny videos on her phone. In the evening, she often went to parties or to the cinema with friends. She usually went to bed at about two o'clock in the morning.

Now Amy has a job. She gets up at a quarter to seven, has a shower and gets dressed. Her work clothes are smart but uncomfortable. She has a quick cup of coffee and walks to the bus stop. There are always lots of people on the bus, so there's nowhere to sit. When Amy gets to work, she's already tired and hungry. The office is very busy and everyone works hard. At lunchtime, Amy eats a sandwich at her desk because there isn't time to leave the office.

Amy usually finishes work at around six thirty, but about once a week she has to work late. She catches the bus and sometimes finds a seat. When she gets home, she has something to eat. She occasionally phones a friend but she often just watches television before going to bed at eleven fifteen. Most of the time she's too tired to go out to the cinema or a restaurant, and her friends don't have parties anymore.

1. *Are students in your country like Amy? How hard do you think they work?*
2. *When do you think is the best age to start your first job?*
3. *What does Amy have for breakfast?*
4. *Why is she tired when she gets to work?*
5. *Why do you think her friends don't have parties anymore?*
6. *Amy isn't very happy. Can you give her any advice?*

MATCH THE OPPOSITES *

easy	nice
disgusting	loudly
horrible	in
start	in front
interesting	answer
quietly	hard
tiny	throw
disagree	come
catch	enormous
ask	hello
out	delicious
goodbye	why
least	slowly
early	most
quickly	late
behind	finish
go	agree
because	boring

(easy ↔ hard)

YOUR FAVOURITE FILM STAR

Answer these questions and then draw his or her face:
1. What colour hair do they have and how long is it?
2. Are their eyes blue, brown, black or a different colour? Don't forget the eyebrows.
3. What shape is their nose? How big is it?
4. Have they got thick lips or thin lips?
5. If the film star is a man, has he got a beard or a moustache?

DIALOGUE: TODAY

Alex: Today...

Toby: What about today?

Alex: Today is a very special day.

Toby: Why? How is it special?

Alex: Today is special because it's the first day of the rest of our lives.

Toby: What's special about that? Every day is the first day of the rest of our lives.

Alex: That's true. And do you know what that means?

Toby: No I don't. What does it mean?

Alex: It means that every day is a very special day.

Toby: Oh go away.

Alex: Why?

Toby: If today is a special day I don't want to spend it with *you*.

WHERE ARE YOU FROM?

country	**nationality**	**capital city**	**language**
United Kingdom	British	London	English

favourite person	**favourite place**
William Shakespeare	Scotland

I'm from the United Kingdom. I'm British. I live in London. I speak English. My favourite famous British person is the writer William Shakespeare (1564 - 1616). My favourite place in the UK is the Highlands of Scotland.

My friend is from China. She's Chinese. She lives in Beijing. She speaks Chinese. Her favourite Chinese person is the poet Li Bai (701 - 762). Her favourite place in China is the island of Hainan.

Write about your country and one other country you know or are interested in:

	country	**nationality**	**capital city**	**language**
1)				
2)				

	favourite person	**favourite place**
1)		
2)		

GETTING READY TO GO OUT? - 1

| hair | body | teeth | to look pretty |

hairbrush, necklace, shaver, toothbrush and toothpaste, shampoo, mirror, soap, makeup, deodorant, comb, earrings, razor,

GETTING READY TO GO OUT? - 2 *

What do you do before you go out? What do your brother and sister do? What do your friends do?

1. She combs her hair.
2. I have a shower and wash my hair.
3. He shaves.
4. They brush their teeth.
5. I put my necklace and earrings on.
6. We put our makeup on.
7. They brush their hair.
8. He puts some deodorant on.
9. You look at yourself in the mirror.

It's almost time to go out! What is everyone doing? **Put the sentences into the present continuous.**

1. She*'s combing her hair.*

SHOES

1. What do women often wear in the Autumn?
2. What can you wear at the beach?
3. What type of shoe is very popular with teenagers, but is also worn by adults when they're not in the office?
4. What can you only wear inside?
5. These shoes are uncomfortable, but women sometimes wear them at parties.
6. These are too cold to wear in the winter.
7. Wear these if the weather's wet and you live in the countryside.

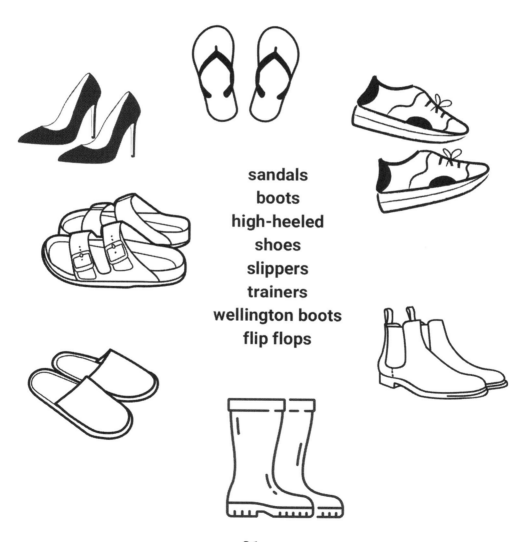

sandals
boots
high-heeled shoes
slippers
trainers
wellington boots
flip flops

REMEMBER THE WORDS - 1

ACROSS
2. twelve a.m.
4. fast
5. noisy
7. there are no hills here, it's ...
9. elephants are big and ...
13. bad, not good
14. use this if you don't want hair on your face
15. help someone to understand

DOWN
1. smaller than a mountain
3. not very often
6. my son is an ... child
8. use this if you don't want to smell
10. impolite
11. comfortable shoes you wear inside
12. You often see daffodils in the spring. They're very ...

WHAT DO YOU DO...?

- What do you do if you're hungry and there's no food in the house?

- What do you do if it's two o'clock in the morning and you can't sleep?

- What does your boss do if you make a mistake at work?

- What do you do if your dog is ill?

- What do you do if your baby starts screaming?

- What do your neighbours do if you have a loud party until three o'clock in the morning?

- What do you do if you're on holiday abroad (in another country) and you lose your passport?

- What does your husband do if you give him an expensive birthday present and he hates it? (or your wife, of course)

AT THE PET SHOP - COMPARATIVES + SUPERLATIVES *

You want to buy a new pet, so you go to the pet shop. The shop only has three animals. Complete these sentences to help you choose the right pet. You need to use **-er** OR **more / less**.

1. The guinea pig is [   ] than the parrot. [cute]
2. The parrot is a bit [   ] than the alligator. [noisy]
3. The alligator is [   ] than the guinea pig. [exciting]
4. The guinea pig is a lot [   ] than the alligator. [dangerous]
5. The alligator is [   ] than the parrot. [intelligent]
6. The parrot is much [   ] than the guinea pig. [old]

So... Which animal do you take home with you?

SAME SOUND, DIFFERENT SPELLING, DIFFERENT MEANING *

Find 6 pairs of words:

ANIMALS – TRUE OR FALSE? *

1. The national animal of Ecuador in South America is the sloth. T / F
2. Slugs don't like the smell of coffee. T / F
3. Ostrich eye are 3 times as big as human eyes. T / F
4. A snail has about fifteen thousand teeth. T / F
5. Scotland's national animal is the kelpie. T / F
6. Kangaroos can't walk (or hop) backwards. T / F
7. There are no snakes in Ireland. T / F
8. Blue whales are about 40 metres long. T / F

Kelpies aren't real, but slugs and snails are, and lots of them live in my garden.

IN YOUR HOUSE OR FLAT...

CAN YOU FIND:

1. A backpack
2. A sofa big enough for three people
3. Something noisy
4. A photo of a baby
5. A green or yellow carpet or rug
6. A digital clock
7. A real flower
8. A table that's not made out of wood
9. A camera (not the camera on your phone)
10. Something that's more than fifty years old
11. A book that makes you laugh
12. A present from your favourite person
13. Something you hate but someone else in your family loves

WHERE? - PREPOSITIONS OF PLACE

Write at least 10 sentences about this room. Include these prepositions of place: above, under, next to, between, in, on, near, in front of, behind

PLAY A GAME - WHERE'S THE CAT?

This is a good game to play when you're with your family in the car.

You have a cat (yes you do). Imagine where the cat is. Make it somewhere unusual. Then the other people in the car ask you questions to find out where the cat is. You can only answer Yes or No.

For example:

You: Where's the cat?

Player 2: Is she in the garden?

You: No she isn't.

Player 3: Is she downstairs?

You: Yes she is.

Player 2: Is she in the living room?

You: Yes she is.

Player 3: Is she on something?

You: No she isn't.

Player 2: Is she under something?

You: Yes she is.

Player 3: Is she under the sofa?

You: No she's not.

Player 2: Is she under the rug?

MY TOWN

My town isn't very big. It has a population of 10,000. But it has everything you need. There are two primary schools and two secondary schools. One of the secondary schools is a private school. There are three supermarkets and lots of smaller shops, so you can buy almost anything you need. There's a library, a gym and a small swimming pool. There isn't a theatre, but there's a little cinema. We have a wonderful park, with a playground for young children.

There's quite a lot to do here. You can join the running club, the rugby club or the book club. You can choose between three different choirs. You can play in the orchestra or the jazz band. Because the town is so small, you can be in the countryside in a few minutes. You can walk in the hills and swim in our local lake.

The thing I like best about my town is the restaurants, cafés and pubs. We have some of the best places to eat and drink in this part of England.

Is there anything you can't find here? Well, I'd like to have a train station. We only have buses. But if we had a train station, house prices would be much higher and I'd probably be living somewhere else.

Write about your village, town or city. *How many schools are there? Are there enough shops? Are there any hospitals? Is there an airport? How much is there to do there? Is it a good place to live?*

SUMMER CAMP   *

Answer the questions:

1. Where is Felton's summer camp this year?
2. Which month is it in?
3. How many days is it on for?
4. Who can go to the camp?
5. How do you register for the camp?
6. What's the best thing children will be able to do at the camp?
7. Will there be anything to eat, and how much will it cost?
8. Does this sound like a good camp? Why / Why not?
9. Do parents need any other information?

DO WHAT I SAY! - THE IMPERATIVE *

You're a primary school teacher and the children in your class are behaving badly. Tell them what to do:

1. Mike is shouting.   **BE QUIET! / STOP SHOUTING!**
2. Emma is looking at her phone.
3. Jim and Judith are playing a game.
4. Alex is standing on his desk.
5. Mary is eating some sweets.
6. Ben is asleep.
7. Mandy has chocolate all over her face.
8. Laurence needs to go to the toilet.
9. Chris is crying.

THE SEASONS *

What's your favourite season, and why? Mine is Autumn. I like cool weather, and I love the stunning yellows, oranges and browns of the countryside in the Autumn.

Decide which words go with which season:

SPRING

SUMMER

AUTUMN

WINTER

freezing, April, camping, snow, cherry, fireworks, chocolate egg, January, sun, cold, tennis, gloves, hot, harvest, beach, Easter, warm, July, present, apple, ice, cherry blossom, ice cream, snowman, holiday, October, lamb, light, picnic, leaf, swimming, skiing, snowball, daffodil, tourist, nuts, Christmas, nest, Halloween, barbecue, dark

CATEGORIES

WRITE DOWN 3:

1. Dangerous animals
2. Cities or towns you like to visit
3. Delicious things to eat
4. Things you did last year
5. People you know who speak very good English
6. Hobbies you think are boring
7. Interesting books
8. Sports you'd like to try
9. Musical instruments
10. Films you think your friends would like
11. English songs
12. Favourite animals
13. Things you find funny
14. Presents you want for Christmas
15. Things you're good at
16. Things you're bad at

CLOTHES *

Which of these clothes are mostly worn by women, which by men and which by both women and men? Be careful with "pants" - use British English.

WOMEN	MEN	BOTH

swimming trunks, leggings, suit, gloves, pants, dungarees, briefs, belt, hoodie, scarf, swimming costume, bra, boxer shorts, tie, top, tights, jumper

PACK A SUITCASE

You're going on holiday for a week.

You can pack twenty-five things. Remember to pack everything you really need, not just clothes.

clothes   shoes   washing things   things to do   and...

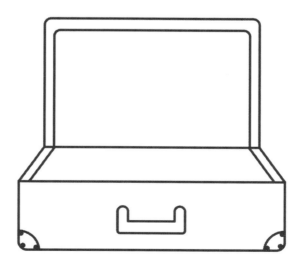

BRITISH OR AMERICAN? *

BRITISH   AMERICAN

block of flats, cookie, pants, trash, parking lot, elevator, pants, car park, torch, rubbish, panties, lift, flashlight, trousers, apartment building, biscuit

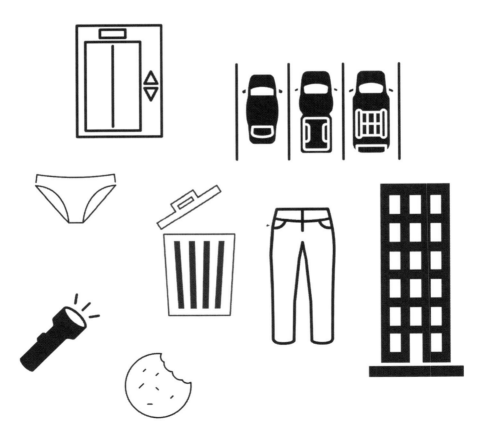

IN THE SALES

You're shopping for clothes in the January sales.

Which of these is:

1) the best deal?

2) the worst deal?

A VERY BAD MONTH *

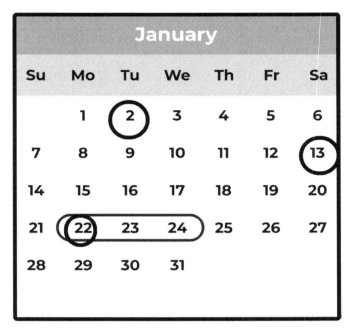

January was a bad month for Jessie.

1. At the beginning of the month she went to the dentist. She had to go to the dentist because she had very bad toothache.
2. A week later she had toothache again. She called the dentist, but he was too busy to see her.
3. She went shopping with her mum that Saturday. Shopping was fun, but she left her purse, which had fifty pounds in it, on the bus.
4. In the fourth week of January she had a car accident. She was in hospital for two nights. The expensive bottle of wine she'd bought for her best friend's birthday was in the car and was broken in the accident.
5. Because she was in hospital Jessie missed her friend's party. But everyone else had a great time.
6. When she got home from hospital Jessie called her dentist again. He was still busy.

1) What was the worst thing that happened to Jessie in January?
2) How often did she call her dentist? When did she call him?
3) What problems do you think she still had at the end of the month?

FURNITURE

PUT THE FURNITURE INTO THE RIGHT ROOMS:

dining room   living room   study / home office   bedroom

cupboard, dining table, coffee table, wardrobe, filing cabinet, bedside table, armchair, chest of drawers, dining chair

WHAT AM I? *

1. I'm alive.
2. I'm not human.
3. I have more than 2 legs.
4. I'm light brown.
5. It's hot where I live.
6. I'm not an insect.
7. I live for a long time, but I'll probably die before you do.
8. I'm probably taller than you are.
9. And I'm several times heavier than you.
10. I help humans.
11. I have hair in my ears. There's a good reason for that.
12. I've worked for humans for a very, very long time.
13. I'm strong.
14. I have wide feet. They help me to walk through sand.
15. I have beautiful long eyelashes. They stop sand from getting into my eyes.
16. I live in the desert.
17. I have one hump on my back.

REMEMBER THE WORDS - 2

```
O T R E S E D Y U N S Y N B O L
H N S I N F O E H S I F D L O G
U R Z I W K Y X K B Z C B V U R
B N X I H C L Y M U T A Y N U I
T M C Q S T U N N I N G U S M O
D O A M H G E H B M O S P G A H
R H R I C X D N A R U I E N R C
A Z T C D R G Q D A V L E I R B
O U B D H H K F L Q M B L G I E
B C O U N T R Y S I D E S G E B
P N A T I O N A L D S M A E D O
U E X P E N S I V E N U X L L R
C L R P L D Q L Q Y Z I O U B D
R O Z V H E I Q Y I T L H M D R
G T S I T N E D Z F P N B E H A
P O U N D E H C A H T O O T B W
```

- the opposite of in front of
- you rarely see one of these
- you can find woods and hills here
- very beautiful
- like trousers, but thinner
- your teeth hurt
- so go and see this person
- use this in the kitchen to put things in
- keep your clothes in this
- you have a husband or wife
- Americans say flashlight
- a hot, dry place
- sleeping
- not cheap
- use this to buy something in the UK
- of a country
- people singing together
- a fish often kept as a pet

PANDA AND DAN *
CAN YOU FILL IN THE GAPS, AND THEN WRITE A FEW MORE SENTENCES TO FINISH THE STORY?

Laura and Andy Bruce are happily ? . They have two children - Dan, who's nine, and Hannah, who's only six. The family has a pet, a beautiful black and white cat called Panda.

Panda is a very lazy cat. He ? most of his time ? on the sofa in the living room. But last Thursday, in the middle of the night, he ? upstairs, raced into Dan's room (Dan always leaves his bedroom door open) and ? onto his bed.

Dan ? straight away. "What are you ? here, Panda?" he ? . "Why aren't you downstairs? Do you want to ? on my bed?" But Panda jumped off the bed and went out of the door.

"He wants me to go with him," ? Dan. "I expect he wants something ? ." He followed Panda to the top of the stairs. And then he ? a light. It was the light of a torch. He ? a noise, too. Two men were ? to each other. One of them had a big bag. Dan saw him ? Dad's expensive laptop and ? it in the bag.

"Oh no," thought Dan. "They ? be burglars. What ? I do?"

must sleep *jumped pick up doing sleeping thought married saw whispering ran heard spends asked shall to eat put woke up*

QUESTIONS WORDS
The 6 Ws and 1 H

Answer the questions:
1. **When** did the accident happen?
2. **Why** are these people arguing?
3. **How** badly hurt is the cyclist?
4. **What** do you think he's saying?
5. **Which** of these two people do you think is responsible for the accident?
6. **Who** should be wearing a helmet?
7. **Where** are the other cars?

SATURDAY NIGHT

What are you doing on Saturday night? Are you going:
- to the cinema?
- to the theatre?
- to a concert?
- to a gig?
- to the opera?
- to the ballet?

Or are you staying at home?

TENSES *

What do you usually do in the evening?
1. I do some work.
2. I phone my parents.
3. I listen to music.
4. I watch television

What's Simon doing at the moment?
1.
2.
3.
4.

What has Anna done today?
1.
2.
3.
4.

What are your friends doing tomorrow?
1.
2.
3.
4.

And when will you have time to go to the cinema with me?
-

SHERLOCK HOLMES *

He's not a real person, but he's perhaps the most famous detective in the world.

Choose the right answers:

1. The Sherlock Holmes stories were written by:
a) Agatha Christie
b) Arthur Conan Doyle
c) Edgar Allan Poe

2. The first Sherlock Holmes story was published in:
a) 1887
b) 1911
c) 1919

3. The great detective lived in London with:
a) His wife and son
b) Nobody - he lived alone
c) Another man

4. Holmes was very good at:
a) Fighting and playing the violin
b) Playing tennis and cooking
c) Singing and acting

5. What was strange about Sherlock Holmes' death?
a) He was killed by his best friend.
b) He was the world's greatest detective, but he was killed by a criminal who was more intelligent than he was.
c) He didn't really die.

LARGE NUMBERS

Practise reading and writing some very large numbers.

100 = a hundred / one hundred

1000 = a thousand / one thousand

1000,000 = a million / one million

123 - a hundred and twenty-three

6,386 - six thousand, three hundred and eighty-six

72,007 - seventy-two thousand and seven.

141, 462 - a hundred and forty-one thousand, four hundred and sixty-two

5,712,254 - five million, seven hundred and twelve thousand, two hundred and fifty-four

Try these ones:

83,422

6,708,275

QUESTIONS WORDS - 2
The 6 Ws and 1 H

Ask and answer 7 questions about the photo:

1. What
2. Where
3. When
4. Who
5. Which
6. Why
7. How

WHEN?

It's two p.m. on Thursday the third of August (the 3rd of August).

Put these words and phrases in the right order:

- today
- a week ago
- six months ago
- in a fortnight
- at the end of the school holidays
- at the moment
- last Friday
- right now
- three weeks from now
- in a few minutes
- this Saturday
- this Autumn
- on the 18th
- in February
- last night
- this second
- next month
- this morning
- next Tuesday
- this evening
- yesterday afternoon
- a couple of days ago
- half an hour ago
- in a week or two
- in a few days
- on New Year's Day
- in an hour
- around Easter time
- in a couple of months
- in the Christmas holidays

A CAMPING TRIP - 1

Last September, Sophie and her boyfriend Oscar decided to go camping. Sophie wanted to find a nice campsite with toilets and hot showers. Oscar thought it would be more fun to go wild camping. He said that using a campsite would be boring, noisy and expensive.

"But is wild camping safe?" asked Sophie.

"Of course it's safe. What are you scared of?" said Oscar.

They took Sophie's car and drove a hundred miles or so into the hills. Then they got out of the car and walked, until they found a good place to put up the tent. They had some food with them, and wanted to cook it over a fire. They found enough wood, but it was too wet to use. So they had a very small, cold supper. It got dark at eight o'clock, so they went to bed early. There was nothing else to do.

It was cold in the tent. In the middle of the night it started to rain and some water got in. Sophie and Oscar both woke up.

"This is horrible," Sophie said. "I want to go home".

"It's just a little bit of water," said Oscar. "And the rain is already stopping. It's fine. It'll probably be hot and sunny tomorrow."

Sophie didn't say anything, because she was listening. She could hear something. She was scared, but she put her head out of the door of the tent. And she saw an enormous dark shape.

"Give me my camera," she whispered.

Sophie has a very good camera. You can see her photo on the next page.

A CAMPING TRIP - 2

This is the photo Sophie took on her and her boyfriend Oscar's camping trip. It's a great photo, isn't it? She has it on the wall of her living room.

- ***Now write the story of the camping trip, if possible without reading it again.***

IRREGULAR VERBS *

Change these verbs from the present simple to the past simple, and from the past simple to the present simple:

PRESENT SIMPLE	PAST SIMPLE
she thinks	she thought
they leave	
she wins	
I see	
they understand	
he drives	
we lose	
I go	
they build	
we choose	
she eats	

PAST SIMPLE	PRESENT SIMPLE
you came	you come
they took	
we got	
we taught	
he wrote	
she said	
they found	
you told	
she sat	
I knew	
they ran	

PRONOUNS *

Use the pronouns to fill the gaps.

"[I] love my life. [I] love my life." [I] say those words to [myself] 30 or 40 times a day, because [I] want to believe [it]. But [my] neighbour's life is so much better than [mine]. [Her] house is really lovely and [she]'s married to a wonderful man - [he]'s a doctor at the hospital, so everyone admires [him]. [He]'s good-looking, too, and of course hospital doctors make lots of money. [I] know [they]'re very intelligent and [they] work hard. But [my] boyfriend and [I] work hard too, and [we] just don't have enough money to buy the basic things [we] need. [We]'re trying to find better jobs, but there aren't many good jobs for people like [us].
[I]'m happy for [them] - for [my] neighbour and [her] perfect husband, [I] mean - but [it]'s not really fair, is [it]? What do [you] think? Do [you] agree with [me]?

I I I I I I I I me myself my my my mine you you he he him she her her it it we we we us they they them them

GOOD HOTEL / BAD HOTEL - 1

James and Samantha talk about hotels they've stayed at.

Samantha: Have you enjoyed the holiday?

James: Of course I have. It's been wonderful. I wish we didn't have to go home tomorrow.

S: I think this is probably the best hotel we've ever stayed at. The enormous bedroom with the king size bed, breakfast on the balcony every morning, the beautiful pool and the sauna room...

J: It's also the most expensive hotel we've ever stayed at. Do you remember our first holiday together, when we were still at university?

S: Oh yes. We stayed at the cheapest hotel we could find. The bed was small and uncomfortable. Breakfast was a cup of tea and a bowl of cereal.

J: There was no swimming pool, obviously. In fact, the shower in our room didn't work.

S: We left after only three nights. I can't remember why.

J: It was because of the cockroaches!

GOOD HOTEL / BAD HOTEL - 2

Write some sentences about these two hotels, or about some hotels that you've stayed at.

HOLIDAY ACCOMMODATION - PROS AND CONS

Where do you stay when you go on holiday? What are the pros and cons? Think of some adjectives.

                                      Pros (good)   **Cons** (bad)

campsite

hostel

holiday cottage

hotel

WHERE SHALL WE GO ON HOLIDAY? - 1

Anne (28) and Robert (27) are friends. They both want to go on holiday this summer, but they don't want to go together, because they went on holiday together last year. Never again! Recommend a good holiday destination for Anne and a different one for Robert, in your country.

ANNE
Likes:
peace and quiet
beauty
art
history
the countryside
swimming
reading
classical music
healthy food
walking
learning new languages

ANNE
Dislikes:
crowds of people
big cities
cars
fast food
pop music
beaches
hot weather
most sport
watching tv

ROBERT
Likes:
sun-bathing
parties
football
hamburgers
the cinema
meeting women
fast cars
alcohol
sleeping
pop music

ROBERT
Dislikes:
children
animals
vegetables
exercise
museums
going to bed early
getting up early
reading
learning languages

WHERE SHALL WE GO ON HOLIDAY? - 2

Thank you for those two recommendations. Anne and Robert are very excited about their holidays. Anne has some questions for you. *Please read her email and write back to her.*

> **Hi!**
> **Thank you very much for suggesting that I go to [   ] this summer. I've never been there. Is it an easy place for tourists to visit? What do you think the weather will be like? Can you give me the name of a quiet hotel that is not too expensive? What is the best museum and the best art gallery? Can I do a trip into the countryside?**
>
> **I'd like to learn some of the language before I go. Is it a difficult language to learn? And can you recommend a good book that I can read in translation?**
>
> **Thank you for your help.**
>
> **From Anne**

ADJECTIVES *

Put the adjectives in the circles in the right order - from low to high. For example: 1) scary, 2) terrifying.

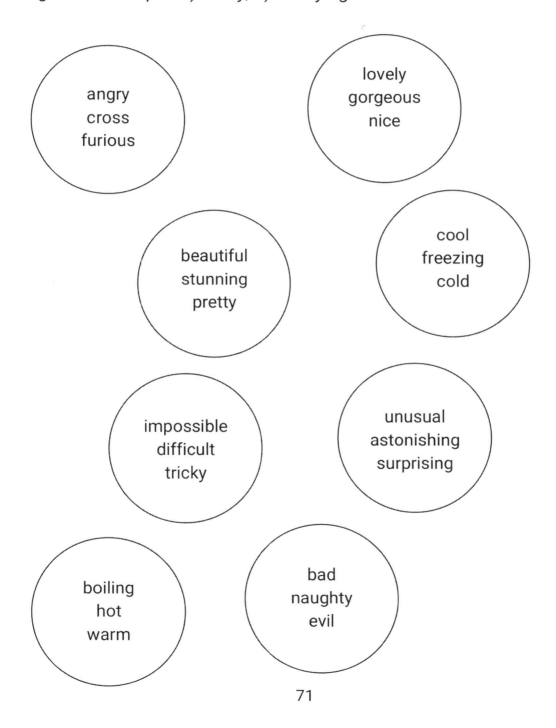

RESEARCH *

Please do some online research in English and find the following information:

1. What is the name of the world's second most translated book?
2. When was it published?
3. Where was it written?
4. What was the illustrator called and what were his other jobs?
5. Which number can you find in the first sentence of the book?
6. Have you ever read the book?
7. If not, would you like to?

WHAT AM I? *

1. A long time ago, I lived in Italy.
2. But I moved to France.
3. Where I live near a pyramid.
4. I'm more popular than you are.
5. Lots of people come to see me.
6. Some people send me love letters.
7. They say I'm very beautiful.
8. I once shared Napoleon's bedroom.
9. But I have my own room now.
10. Are you a millionaire? You can't buy me.
11. I went back to Italy in 1911.
12. For 2 years, no-one could find me.
13. Then they took me back home.
14. I live in an enormous building in a beautiful city.
15. There are thousands of things to see here.
16. But most people just want to see me.
17. Is it because of my special smile?

DIFFERENT PEOPLE, DIFFERENT PETS - 1

Recommend a suitable pet for each of these people:

- Patrick is seventy-eight. He lives by himself in a small house with a very small garden. He likes going for a short walk every day. He doesn't want to die before his pet does.

- Jenny is twenty-one. She lives with some friends in a flat in London. She has just started her first job and is very busy.

- Tim is ten. He lives with his parents and his two younger sisters in a big house with a big garden in the middle of the countryside. His dad works from home.

- You.

- A friend who has young children.

DIFFERENT PEOPLE, DIFFERENT PETS - 2

You receive a message from your friend who has young children:

> Thank you for recommending a pet. It was nice of you and I liked your idea, but in the end I decided to get a bigger and more exciting pet. The children love it! Here's a photo of the new pet with my youngest child. They're already good friends.

- *Write an email to your friend.*

DIRECTIONS

Do you know how to read a compass in English?

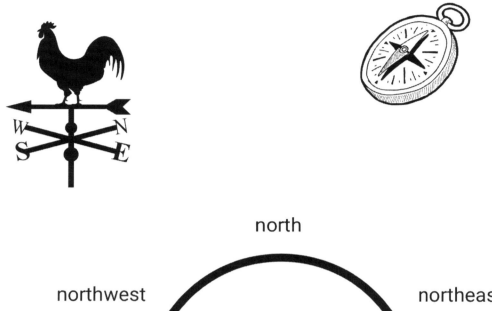

north

northwest northeast

west east

southwest southeast

south

DIRECTIONS - THE UNITED KINGDOM

Scotland is in the north, Northern Ireland is in the northwest, Wales is in the west and England is in the south of the United Kingdom.

Can you name their capital cities?

FLABEST
NOLDNO
FRICAFD
BUNDREIGH

POSTCARD

You're on holiday in Tallinn, the capital of Estonia. Write a postcard to a friend in the UK. (If you've never been to Tallinn, you'll need to do a little bit of research).

PERSONALITY - OPPOSITE ADJECTIVES *

These are all negative words. What are the opposite, positive words?

NEGATIVE	POSITIVE
nasty	
dishonest	
unfriendly	
rude	
unambitious	
impolite	
vain	
unhelpful	
stupid	
boring	
impatient	
thoughtless	
lazy	
uncreative	
selfish	
arrogant	
unkind	
pessimistic	

PEOPLE

Think of 6 adjectives to describe each of these people:

1)
2)
3)
4)
5)
6)

1)
2)
3)
4)
5)
6)

BAD BOSS / GOOD TEACHER

Describe this boss and this teacher. Then describe your boss or teacher.

- What does he or she look like?
- What does he or she usually wear? And what is he or she wearing today?
- What is he or she like?

MY FRIEND

Chris remembers his best friend at primary school:

I had three school friends. I liked all of them and we had fun together, but Patrick was my best friend. He was a tall boy, with short brown hair and blue eyes. He didn't say much, but he listened. So he knew when one of us was feeling bad. One time, when we were eight or nine, I got to school late because I was tired and didn't want to get up, didn't want to go to school. When the teacher saw me, she began to shout at me. She said I was lazy. I started to cry, but Patrick sat next to me in the classroom and told me not to worry. He gave me some chocolate, too. I felt a bit better after that. After school we went to the park and he taught me how to climb the big tree. And then life was good again.

Which verb isn't in the past simple?

Now write a few sentences about a friend from your past. Use the past simple.

GRAMMAR *

Find 1 of each:

1. A noun
2. A comparative
3. A verb
4. An adjective
5. A superlative
6. A capital letter
7. An adverb
8. A pronoun
9. A preposition
10. An irregular plural
11. An article

Millie isn't my best friend, but she's a lot nicer than Emma is. In our maths lesson yesterday the teacher asked me a difficult question. I didn't know the answer, and some of the other children laughed at me. Millie smiled at me, but Emma laughed loudly and didn't stop until the teacher told her to.

DESIGN YOUR NEW HOUSE - 1

There are ten rooms and a hall downstairs and twelve rooms and a corridor upstairs. There's lots of space in the cellar and in the attic. There's a large garden.

You can choose from:

master bedroom	music room
single bedroom	storage room
double bedroom	wine cellar
guest room	games room
bathroom	home cinema
toilet	indoor swimming pool
dining room	home gym
living room	snug / den
second living room / family room	sunroom
kitchen	library
utility room	conservatory
study / home office	single garage
playroom	double garage

DESIGN YOUR NEW HOUSE - 2

Write some sentences.

Example sentences:

I'd like to have a gym but I don't want a swimming pool.

I'd rather have a guest room than a third bathroom.

I don't think I need a games room.

A home cinema would be nice.

Who needs a sun room?

Two bathrooms are enough.

A second living room might be nice.

It's important to have a dining room.

Then draw your floor plans for downstairs and upstairs. Is this your dream house? Is it big enough?

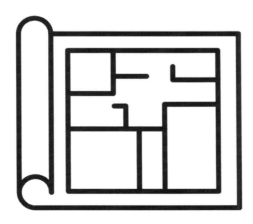

AN EMPTY ROOM

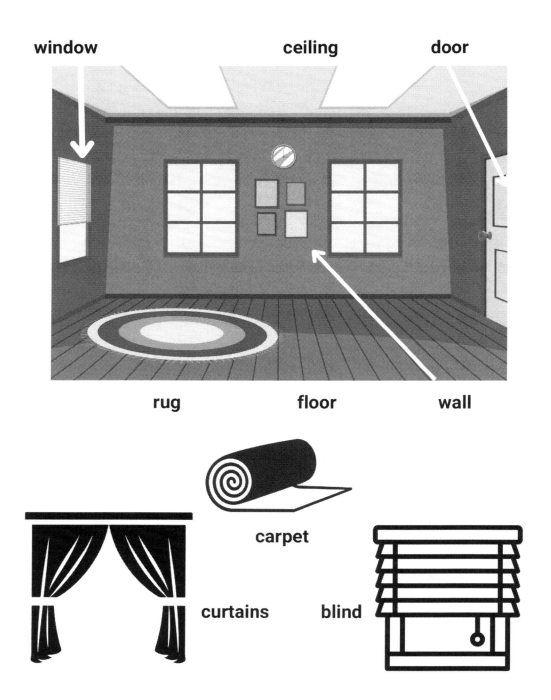

IDIOMS

You can speak good English without using idioms. But it's helpful if you can understand them.

Here are some idioms people sometimes use to say that something is **EASY**:

Alberto: I'm worried about the English exam tomorrow.

Julia: Why? You're very good at English. It'll be ***a walk in the park***.

Alberto: If I don't pass the exam, I won't be able to go to the university I want.

Julia: It's only an intermediate level exam. Intermediate level English isn't ***rocket science***, is it? You could pass an exam like that ***with your eyes shut***.

Rocket science is hard. Please don't try to do it with your eyes shut.

THE GOLDFISH AND THE KITTEN

Look at the photos and tell the story:

REMEMBER THE WORDS - 3

ACROSS
1. a very rich person
3. a lot of people in one place
4. to think someone is great
5. sleep in a tent
6. under your feet in a house
7. very surprising
10. a pop concert
11. by yourself
12. he thinks he's something special

DOWN
1. go here to see very old things
2. a room made out of glass
3. inside, above your head
5. you can find him in prison
8. a room in your house where you work
9. it / she

SOLUTIONS

CONTINENTS
1) South America, Australia, Africa, Europe, North America, Asia 2) 3, 3) Asia, Africa, 4) Asia, 5) Australia, 6) Africa, 7) Europe, 8) European, 9) Australia or North America

ODD ONE OUT
1) lamb, 2) boring, 3) Egypt, 4) story, 5) swim, 6) Brazil, 7) broccoli, 8) pretty, 9) spider, 10) beer, 11) bike, 12) hit, 13) custard, 14) fox, 15) large, 16) shout, 17) shark, 18) trousers

ANDREW'S FAMILY
1) F, 2) F, 3) T, 4) T, 5) F, 6) F, 7) F

WHAT TIME IS IT?

It's a quarter past one	It's 1:15 - one fifteen
It's ten to nine	It's 8:50 - eight fifty
It's twenty-five past seven	It's 7:25 - seven twenty-five
It's twenty to four	It's 3:40 - three forty
It's five past two	It's 2:05 - two oh five
It's six minutes to six	It's 5:54 - five fifty-four
It's a quarter to eight	It's 7:45 - seven forty-five
It's ten past nine	It's 9:10 - nine ten
It's half past five in the morning	It's 5:30 a.m. - five thirty a.m.
It's twelve o'clock / midnight	It's 12 - twelve / midnight
It's three minutes past three	It's 3:03 - three oh three
It's seven o'clock in the evening	It's 7 p.m. - seven p.m.

WHAT TIME?
He has breakfast at..., He starts work at..., He goes to the supermarket at..., He walks his dog at..., He has dinner at... He watches television at..., He goes to bed at...

MATCH THE OPPOSITES
disgusting / delicious, horrible / nice, start / finish, interesting / boring, quietly / loudly, tiny / enormous, disagree/ agree, catch / throw, ask / answer, out / in, goodbye / hello, least / most, early / late, quickly / slowly, behind / in front, go / come, because / why

GETTING READY TO GO OUT? - 2
2) I'm having a shower and washing my hair. 3) He's shaving. 4) They're brushing their teeth. 5) I'm putting my necklace and earrings on. 6) We're putting our makeup on. 7) They're brushing their hair. 8) He's putting some deodorant on. 9) You're looking at yourself in the mirror.

AT THE PET SHOP
1) cuter, 2) noisier, 3) more exciting, 4) less dangerous, 5) less intelligent, 6) older

SAME SOUND, DIFFERENT SPELLING, DIFFERENT MEANING
see / sea, pair / pear, meat / meet, flower / flour, hare / hair, write / right

ANIMALS - TRUE OR FALSE?
1) F, 2) T, 3) F, 4) T, 5) F, 6) T, 7) T, 8) F

SUMMER CAMP
1) It's at Felton Primary School. 2) It's in August. 3) It's on for six days.
4) Children aged 4 to 11. 5) You register online.
7) Yes, lunch is included. We don't know how much it will cost.
9) They need to know how much the camp will cost and the daily start and finish times.

DO WHAT I SAY!
2) Put your phone away. Stop looking at your phone.
3) Put that game away. Stop playing that game.
4) Get off your desk. Sit down.
5) Take that sweet out of your mouth. Stop eating those sweets. Give me those sweets.
6) Wake up.
7) Go and wash your face.
8) Go to the toilet.
9) Stop crying.

THE SEASONS
Spring: April, chocolate egg, Easter, warm, cherry blossom, lamb, daffodil, nest
Summer: camping, cherry, sun, tennis, hot, beach, July, ice cream, holiday, light, picnic, swimming, tourist, barbecue
Autumn: harvest, apple, October, leaf, nuts, Halloween
Winter: freezing, snow, fireworks, January, cold, gloves, present, ice, snowman, skiing, snowball, Christmas, dark

CLOTHES
Women: leggings, pants, swimming costume, bra, tights
Men: swimming trunks, suit, briefs, boxer shorts, tie
Both: gloves, dungarees, belt, hoodie, scarf, top, jumper

BRITISH OR AMERICAN?
lift / elevator, car park / parking lot, pants / panties, rubbish / trash, trousers / pants, block of flats / apartment building, torch / flashlight, biscuit / cookie

A VERY BAD MONTH
1) She had quite a serious car accident.
2) She called him three times. She called him to book an appointment, which was on the second of January. She called him again a week later, on around the 9th of January, and she called him a third time when she got home from hospital on the 24th of January.
3) She was probably still recovering from her accident and she still had toothache. Losing fifty pounds may have caused her some problems too.

WHAT AM I?
A dromedary

PANDA AND DAN
Laura and Andy Bruce are happily married. They have two children - Dan, who's nine, and Hannah, who's only six. The family has a pet, a beautiful black and white cat called Panda.
Panda is a very lazy cat. He spends most of his time sleeping on the sofa in the living room. But last Thursday, in the middle of the night, he ran upstairs, raced into Dan's room (Dan always leaves his bedroom door open) and jumped onto his bed.
Dan woke up straight away. "What are you doing here, Panda?" he asked. "Why aren't you downstairs? Do you want to sleep on my bed?" But Panda jumped off the bed and went out of the door.
"He wants me to go with him," thought Dan. "I expect he wants something to eat." He followed Panda to the top of the stairs. And then he saw a light. It was the light of a torch. He heard a noise, too. Two men were whispering to each other. One of them had a big bag. Dan saw him pick up Dad's expensive laptop and put it in the bag.
"Oh no," thought Dan. "They must be burglars. What shall I do?"

TENSES
He's doing some work. He's phoning his parents. He's listening to music. He's watching television.
She's done some work. She's phoned her parents. She's listened to music. She's watched television.
They're doing some work. They're phoning their parents. They're listening to music. They're watching television.
I'll probably have time to go to the cinema with you on Thursday.

SHERLOCK HOLMES
1) b, 2) a, 3) c, 4) a, 5) c

IRREGULAR VERBS
they left, she won, I saw, they understood, he drove, we lost, I went, they built, we chose, she ate
they take, we get, we teach, he writes, she says, they find, you tell, she sits, I know, they run

PRONOUNS

"I love my life. I love my life." I say those words to myself 30 or 40 times a day, because I want to believe them. But my neighbour's life is so much better than mine. Her house is really lovely and she's married to a wonderful man - he's a doctor at the hospital, so everyone admires him. He's good-looking, too, and of course hospital doctors make lots of money. I know they're very intelligent and they work hard. But my boyfriend and I work hard too, and we just don't have enough money to buy the basic things we need. We're trying to find better jobs, but there aren't many good jobs for people like us.
I'm happy for them - for my neighbour and her perfect husband, I mean - but it's not really fair, is it? What do you think? Do you agree with me?

ADJECTIVES

cross, angry, furious - nice, lovely, gorgeous - pretty, beautiful, stunning - cool, cold, freezing - tricky, difficult, impossible - unusual, surprising, astonishing - warm, hot, boiling - naughty, bad, evil

RESEARCH
1) Le Petit Prince.
2) In 1943.
3) In New York.
4) Antoine de Saint-Exupéry. He was also a pilot and a writer.
5) 6

WHAT AM I?
The Mona Lisa.

PERSONALITY - OPPOSITE ADJECTIVES

nasty / nice, dishonest / honest, unfriendly / friendly, rude / polite, unambitious / ambitious, impolite / polite, vain / modest, unhelpful / helpful, stupid / intelligent, boring / interesting, impatient / patient, thoughtless / thoughtful, lazy / hardworking, uncreative / creative, selfish / unselfish, arrogant / modest, unkind / kind, pessimistic / optimistic

GRAMMAR - for example:
Noun - teacher   Comparative - nicer   Verb - to ask   Adjective - difficult
Superlative - best   Capital letter - W   Adverb - loudly   Pronoun - me
Preposition - at   Irregular plural - children   Article - the

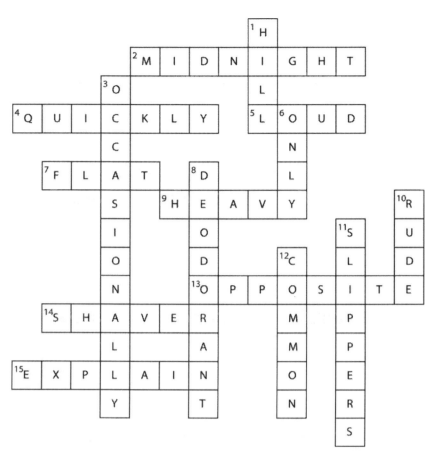

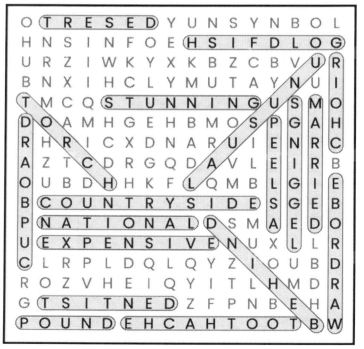

Across:
1. MILLIONAIRE
3. CROWD
4. ADMIRE
5. CAMP
6. FLOOR
7. ASTONISHING
10. GIG
11. ALONE
12. ARROGANT

Down:
1. MUSEUM
2. CONSERVATRY
3. CRIMING
5. CAMPALL (CRIMINAL)
7. ASTORY
8. STUDY
9. PROUND

Printed in France by Amazon
Brétigny-sur-Orge, FR